THE DOCTRINE

OF FASCISM

by BENITO MUSSOLINI

First Edition

19 18 17 16 15 / 10 9 8 7 6 5 4 3 2 1

Benito Amilcare Andrea Mussolini
(29 July 1883 – 28 April 1945)
was an Italian politician who led the National Fascist
Party, ruling the country from 1922 to his ousting in
1943, and is credited with being one of the key figures
in the creation of fascism.

(This article, co-written by Giovanni Gentile, is considered to be the most complete articulation of Mussolini's political views. This is the only <u>complete</u> official translation copied directly from an official Fascist government publication of 1935, *Fascism Doctrine and Institutions,* by Benito Mussolini, Ardita Publishers, Rome, pages 7-42. This translation includes all the <u>endnotes</u> from the original.)

The Doctrine Of Fascism

Like all sound political conceptions, Fascism is action and it is thought; action in which doctrine is immanent, and doctrine arising from a given system of historical forces in which it is inserted, and working on them from within [1]. It has therefore a form correlated to contingencies of time and space; but it has also an ideal content which makes it an expression of truth in the higher region of the history of thought [2]. There is no way of exercising a spiritual influence in the world as a human will dominating the will of others, unless one has a conception both of the transient and the specific reality on which that action is to be exercised, and of the permanent and universal reality in which the transient dwells and has its being. To know men one must know man; and to know man one must be acquainted with reality and its laws. There can be no conception of the State which is not fundamentally a conception of life: philosophy or intuition, system of ideas evolving within the framework of logic or concentrated in a vision or a faith, but always, at least potentially, an organic conception of the world.

Thus many of the practical expressions of Fascism such as party organization, system of education, and discipline can only be understood when considered in relation to its general attitude toward life. A spiritual attitude [3]. Fascism sees in the world not only those superficial, material aspects in which man appears as an individual, standing by himself, self-centere**d, subject to natural law, which instinctively urges him toward a life of selfish momentary pleasure; it sees not only the individual but the nation and the country; individuals and generations bound together by a moral law, with common traditions and a mission which suppressing the instinct for life closed in a brief circle of pleasure, builds up a higher life, founded on duty, a life free from the limitations of time and space, in which the individual, by self-sacrifice, the renunciation of self-interest, by death itself, can achieve that purely spiritual existence in which his value as a man consists.

The conception is therefore a spiritual one, arising from the general reaction of the century against the materialistic positivism of the XIXth century. Anti-positivistic but positive; neither skeptical nor agnostic; neither pessimistic nor supinely optimistic as are, generally speaking, the doctrines (all negative) which place the center of life outside man; whereas, by the exercise of his free will, man can and must create his own world.

Fascism wants man to be active and to engage in action with all his energies; it wants him to be manfully aware of the difficulties besetting him and ready to face them. It conceives of life as a struggle in which it behooves a man to win for himself a really worthy place, first of all by fitting himself (physically, morally, intellectually) to become the implement required for winning it. As for the individual, so for the nation, and so for mankind [4]. Hence the high value of culture in all its forms (artistic, religious, scientific) [5] and the outstanding importance of education. Hence also the essential value of work, by which man subjugates nature and creates the human world (economic, political, ethical, and intellectual).

This positive conception of life is obviously an ethical one. It invests the whole field of reality as well as the human activities which master it. No action is exempt from moral judgment; no activity can be despoiled of the value which a moral purpose confers on all things. Therefore life, as conceived of by the Fascist, is serious, austere, and religious; all its manifestations are poised in a world sustained by moral forces and subject to spiritual responsibilities. The Fascist disdains an "easy" life [6].

The Fascist conception of life is a religious one [7], in which man is viewed in his immanent relation to a higher law, endowed with an objective will transcending the in-dividual and raising him to conscious membership of a spiritual society. "Those who perceive nothing beyond opportunistic considerations in the religious policy of the Fascist regime fail to realize that Fascism is not only a system of government but also and above all a system of thought.

In the Fascist conception of history, man is man only by virtue of the spiritual process to which he contributes as a member of the family, the social group, the nation, and in function of history to which all nations bring their contribution. Hence the great

value of tradition in records, in language, in customs, in the rules of social life [8]. Outside history man is a nonentity. Fascism is therefore opposed to all individualistic abstractions based on eighteenth century materialism; and it is opposed to all Jacobinistic utopias and innovations. It does not believe in the possibility of "happiness" on earth as conceived by the economistic literature of the XVIIIth century, and it therefore rejects the theological notion that at some future time the human family will secure a final settlement of all its difficulties. This notion runs counter to experience which teaches that life is in continual flux and in process of evolution. In politics Fascism aims at realism; in practice it desires to deal only with those problems which are the spontaneous product of historic conditions and which find or suggest their own solutions [9]. Only by entering in to the process of reality and taking possession of the forces at work within it, can man act on man and on nature [10].

Anti-individualistic, the Fascist conception of life stresses the importance of the State and accepts the individual only in so far as his interests coincide with those of the State, which stands for the conscience and the universal, will of man as a historic entity [11]. It is opposed to classical liberalism which arose as a reaction to absolutism and exhausted its historical function when the State became the expression of the conscience and will of the people. Liberalism denied the State in the name of the individual; Fascism reasserts

The rights of the State as expressing the real essence of the individual [12]. And if liberty is to he the attribute of living men and not of abstract dummies invented by individualistic liberalism, then Fascism stands for liberty, and for the only liberty worth having, the liberty of the State and of the individual within the State [13]. The Fascist conception of the State is all embracing; outside of it no human or spiritual values can exist, much less have value. Thus understood, Fascism, is totalitarian, and the Fascist State - a synthesis and a unit inclusive of all values - interprets, develops, and potentates the whole life of a people [14].

No individuals or groups (political parties, cultural associations, economic unions, social classes) outside the State [15]. Fascism is therefore opposed to Socialism to which unity within the State (which amalgamates classes into a single economic and ethical reality) is unknown, and which sees in history nothing but the class struggle. Fascism is likewise opposed to trade unionism as a class weapon. But when brought within the orbit of the State, Fascism recognizes the real needs which gave rise to socialism and trade unionism, giving them due weight in the guild or corporative system in which divergent interests are coordinated and harmonized in the unity of the State [16].

Grouped according to their several interests, individuals form classes; they form trade-unions when organized according to their several economic activities; but first and foremost they form the State, which is no mere matter of numbers, the suns of the individuals forming the majority. Fascism is therefore opposed to that form of democracy which equates a nation to the majority, lowering it to the level of the largest number [17]; but it is the purest form of democracy if the nation be considered as it should be from the point of view of quality rather than quantity, as an idea, the mightiest because the most ethical, the most coherent, the truest, expressing itself in a people as the conscience and will of the few, if not, indeed, of one, and ending to express itself in the conscience and the will of the mass, of the whole group ethnically molded by natural and historical conditions into a nation, advancing, as one conscience and one will, along the self same line of development and spiritual formation [18]. Not a race, nor a geographically defined region, but a people, historically perpetuating itself; a multitude unified by an idea and imbued with the will to live, the will to power, self-consciousness, personality [19].

In so far as it is embodied in a State, this higher personality becomes a nation. It is not the nation which generates the State; that is an antiquated naturalistic concept which afforded a basis for XIXth century publicity in favor of national governments. Rather is it the State which creates the nation, conferring volition and therefore real life on a people made aware of their moral unity.

The right to national independence does not arise from any merely literary and idealistic form of self-consciousness; still less from a more or less passive and unconscious *de facto* situation, but from an active, self-conscious, political will expressing itself in action and ready to prove its rights. It arises, in short, from the existence, at least *in fieri,* of a State. Indeed, it is the State which, as the expression of a universal ethical will, creates the right to national independence [20].

A nation, as expressed in the State, is a living, ethical entity only in so far as it is progressive. Inactivity is death. Therefore the State is not only Authority which governs and confers legal form and spiritual value on individual wills, but it is also Power which makes its will felt and respected beyond its own frontiers, thus affording practical proof of the universal character of the decisions necessary to ensure its development. This implies organization and expansion, potential if not actual. Thus the State equates itself to the will of man, whose development cannot he checked by obstacles and which, by achieving self-expression, demonstrates its infinity [21].

The Fascist State , as a higher and more powerful expression of personality, is a force, but a spiritual one. It sums up all the manifestations of the moral and intellectual life of man. Its functions cannot therefore be limited to those of enforcing order and keeping the peace, as the liberal doctrine had it. It is no mere mechanical device for defining the sphere within which the individual may duly exercise his supposed rights. The Fascist State is an inwardly accepted standard and rule of conduct, a discipline of the whole person; it permeates the will no less than the intellect. It stands for a principle which becomes the central motive of man as a member of civilized society, sinking deep down into his personality; it dwells in the heart of the man of action and of the thinker, of the artist and of the man of science: soul of the soul [22].

Fascism, in short, is not only a law-giver and a founder of institutions, but an educator and a promoter of spiritual life. It aims at refashioning not only the forms of life but their content - man, his character, and his faith. To achieve this propose it enforces discipline and uses authority, entering into the soul and ruling with undisputed sway. Therefore it has chosen as its emblem the Lictor's rods, the symbol of unity, strength, and justice.

POLITICAL AND SOCIAL DOCTRINE

When in the now distant March of 1919, speaking through the columns of the *Popolo d'Italia* I summoned to Milan the surviving interventionists who had intervened, and who had followed me ever since the foundation of the Fascist of revolutionary action in January 1915, I had in mind no specific doctrinal program. The only doctrine of which I had practical experience was that of socialism, from until the winter of 1914 - nearly a decade. My experience was that both of a follower and a leader but it was not doctrinal experience. My doctrine during that period had been the doctrine of action. A uniform, universally accepted doctrine of Socialism had not existed since 1905, when the revisionist movement, headed by Bernstein, arose in Germany, countered by the formation, in the see-saw of tendencies, of a left revolutionary movement which in Italy never quitted the field of phrases, whereas, in the case of Russian socialism, it became the prelude to Bolshevism.

Reformism, revolutionism, centrism, the very echo of that terminology is dead, while in the great river of Fascism one can trace currents which had their source in Sorel, Peguy,

Lagardelle of the *Movement Socialists,* and in the cohort of Italian syndicalist who from 1904 to 1914 brought a new note into the Italian socialist environment - previously emasculated and chloroformed by fornicating with Giolitti's party - a note sounded in Olivetti's *Pagine Libere,* Orano's *Lupa,* Enrico Leone's *Divenirs Socials.*

When the war ended in 1919 Socialism, as a doctrine, was already dead; it continued to exist only as a grudge, especially in Italy where its only chance lay in inciting to reprisals against the men who had willed the war and who were to be made to pay for it.

The *Popolo d'Italia* described itself in its subtitle as the daily organ of fighters and producers. The word producer was already the expression of a mental trend. Fascism was not the nursling of a doctrine previously drafted at a desk; it was born of the need of action, and was action; it was not a party but, in the first two years, an anti-party and a movement. The name I gave the organization fixed its character.

Yet if anyone cares to reread the now crumpled sheets of those days giving an account of the meeting at which the Italian *Fasci di combattimento* were founded, he will find not a doctrine but a series of pointers, forecasts, hints which, when freed from the inevitable matrix of contingencies, were to develop in a few years time into a series of doctrinal positions entitling Fascism to rank as a political doctrine differing from all others, past or present.

"If the bourgeoisie - I then said - believe that they have found in us their lightening-conductors, they arc mistaken. We must go towards the people... We wish the working classes to accustom themselves to the responsibilities of management so that they may realize that it is no easy matter to run a business... We will fight both technical and spiritual rear-guirdism... Now that the succession of the regime is open we must not be fainthearted. We must rush forward; if the present regime is to be superseded we must take its place. The right of succession is ours, for we urged the country to enter the war and we led it to victory... The existing forms of political representation cannot satisfy us; we want direst representation of the several interests... It may be objected that this program implies a return to the guilds (corporazioni). No matter!· I therefore hope this assembly will accept the economic claims advanced by national syndicalism ...

Is it not strange that from the very first day, at Piazza San Sepolcro, the word "guild" (corporazione) was pronounced, a word which, as the Revolution developed, was to express one of the basic legislative and social creations of the regime?

The years preceding the March on Rome cover a period during which the need of action forbade delay and careful doctrinal elaborations. Fighting was going on in the towns and villages. There were discussions but... there was something more sacred and more important... death... Fascists knew how to die. A doctrine - fully elaborated, divided up into chapters and paragraphs with annotations, may have been lacking, but it was replaced by something far m :) re decisive, - by a faith. All the same, if with the help of books, articles, resolutions passed at congresses, major and minor speeches, anyone should care to revive the memory of those days, he will find, provided he knows how to seek and select, that the doctrinal foundations were laid while the battle was still raging. Indeed, it was during those years that Fascist thought armed, refined itself, and proceeded ahead with its organization. The problems of the individual and the State; the problems of authority and liberty; political, social, and more especially national problems were discussed; the conflict with liberal, democratic, socialistic, Masonic doctrines and with those of the *Partito Popolare,* was carried on at the same time as the punitive expeditions. Nevertheless, the lack of a formal system was used by disingenuous adversaries as an argument for proclaiming Fascism incapable of elaborating a doctrine at the very time when that doctrine was being formulated - no matter how tumultuously, - first, as is the case with all new ideas, in the guise of violent dogmatic negations; then in the more positive guise of constructive theories, subsequently incorporated, in 1926, *1927,* and 1928, in the laws and institutions of the regime.

Fascism is now clearly defined not only as a regime but as a doctrine. This means that Fascism, exercising its critical faculties on itself and on others, has studied from its own special standpoint and judged by its own standards all the problems affecting the material and intellectual interests now causing such grave anxiety to the nations of the world, and is ready to deal with them by its own policies. First of all, as regards the future development of mankind, and quite apart from all present political considerations. Fascism does not, generally speaking, believe in the possibility or utility of perpetual peace. It therefore discards pacifism as a cloak for cowardly supine renunciation in contradistinction to self-sacrifice. War alone keys up all human energies to their maximum tension and sets the seal of nobility on those peoples who have the courage to face it. All other tests are substitutes which never place a man face to face with himself before the alternative of life or death. Therefore all doctrines which postulate peace at all costs are incompatible with Fascism. Equally foreign to the spirit of Fascism, even if accepted as useful in meeting special political situations -- are all internationalistic or League superstructures which, as history shows, crumble to the ground whenever the heart of nations is deeply stirred by sentimental, idealistic or practical considerations. Fascism carries this anti-pacifistic attitude into the life of the individual. " I don't care a damn „ *(me ne frego)* - the proud motto of the fighting squads scrawled by a wounded man on his bandages, is not only an act of philosophic stoicism, it sums up a doctrine which is not merely political: it is evidence of a fighting spirit which accepts all risks. It signifies new style of Italian life. The Fascist accepts and loves life; he rejects and despises suicide as cowardly. Life as he understands it means duty, elevation, conquest; life must be lofty and full, it must be lived for oneself but above all for others, both near bye and far off, present and future.

The population policy of the regime is the consequence of these premises. The Fascist loves his neighbor, but the word neighbor "does not stand for some vague and unseizable conception. Love of one's neighbor does not exclude necessary educational severity; still less does it exclude differentiation and rank. Fascism will have nothing to do with universal embraces; as a member of the community of nations it looks other peoples straight in the eyes; it is vigilant and on its guard; it follows others in all their manifestations and notes any changes in their interests; and it does not allow itself to be deceived by mutable and fallacious appearances.

Such a conception of life makes Fascism the resolute negation of the doctrine underlying so-called scientific and Marxian socialism, the doctrine of historic materialism which would explain the history of mankind in terms of the class struggle and by changes in the processes and instruments of production, to the exclusion of all else.

That the vicissitudes of economic life - discoveries of raw materials, new technical processes, and scientific inventions - have their importance, no one denies; but that they suffice to explain human history to the exclusion of other factors is absurd. Fascism believes now and always in sanctity and heroism, that is to say in acts in which no economic motive - remote or immediate - is at work. Having denied historic materialism, which sees in men mere puppets on the surface of history, appearing and disappearing on the crest of the waves while in the depths the real directing forces move and work, Fascism also denies the immutable and irreparable character of the class struggle which is the natural outcome of this economic conception of history; above all it denies that the class struggle is the preponderating agent in

social transformations. Having thus struck a blow at socialism in the two main points of its doctrine, all that remains of it is the sentimental aspiration-old as humanity itself-toward social relations in which the sufferings and sorrows of the humbler folk will be alleviated. But here again Fascism rejects the economic interpretation of felicity as something to be secured socialistically, almost automatically, at a given stage of economic evolution when all will be assured a maximum of material comfort. Fascism denies the materialistic conception of happiness as a possibility, and abandons it to the economists of the mid-eighteenth century. This means that Fascism denies the equation: well-being = happiness, which sees in men mere animals, content when they can feed and fatten, thus reducing them to a vegetative existence pure and simple.

After socialism, Fascism trains its guns on the whole block of democratic ideologies, and rejects both their premises and their practical applications and implements. Fascism denies that numbers, as such, can be the determining factor in human society; it denies the right of numbers to govern by means of periodical consultations; it asserts the irremediable and fertile and beneficent inequality of men who cannot be leveled by any such mechanical and extrinsic device as universal suffrage. Democratic regimes may be described as those under which the people are, from time to time, deluded into the belief that they exercise sovereignty, while all the time real sovereignty resides in and is exercised by other and sometimes irresponsible and secret forces. Democracy is a kingless regime infested by many kings who are sometimes more exclusive, tyrannical, and destructive than one, even if he be a tyrant. This explains why Fascism - although, for contingent reasons, it was republican in tendency prior to 1922 - abandoned that stand before the March on Rome, convinced that the form of government is no longer a matter of preeminent importance, and because the study of past and present monarchies and past and present republics shows that neither monarchy nor republic can be judged *sub specie aeternitatis,* but that each stands for a form of government expressing the political evolution, the history, the traditions, and the psychology of a given country.

Fascism has outgrown the dilemma: monarchy v. republic, over which democratic regimes too long dallied, attributing all insufficiencies to the former and proning the latter as a regime of perfection, whereas experience teaches that some republics are inherently reactionary and absolutist while some monarchies accept the most daring political and social experiments.

In one of his philosophic Meditations Renan - who had prefascist intuitions remarks, "Reason and science are the products of mankind, but it is chimerical to seek reason directly for the people and through the people. It is not essential to the existence of reason that all should be familiar with it; and even if all had to be initiated, this could not be achieved through democracy which seems fated to lead to the extinction of all arduous forms of culture and all highest forms of learning. The maxim that society exists only for the well-being and freedom of the individuals composing it does not seem to be in conformity with nature's plans, which care only for the species and seem ready to sacrifice the individual. It is much to be feared that the last word of democracy thus understood (and let me hasten to add that it is susceptible of a different interpretation) would be a form of society in which a degenerate mass would have no thought beyond that of enjoying the ignoble pleasures of the vulgar ".

In rejecting democracy Fascism rejects the absurd conventional lie of political equalitarianism, the habit of collective irresponsibility, the myth of felicity and indefinite progress. But if democracy be understood as meaning a regime in which the masses are not driven back to the margin of the State, and then the writer of these pages has already defined Fascism as an organized, centralized, authoritarian democracy.

Fascism is definitely and absolutely opposed to the doctrines of liberalism, both in the political and the economic sphere. The importance of liberalism in the XIXth century should not be exaggerated for present day polemical purposes, nor should we make of one of the many doctrines which flourished in that century a religion for mankind for the present and for all time to come. Liberalism really flourished for fifteen years only. It arose in 1830 as a reaction to the Holy Alliance which tried to force Europe to recede further back than 1789; it touched its zenith in 1848 when even Pius IXth was a liberal. Its decline began immediately after that year. If 1848 was a year of light and poetry, 1849 was a year of darkness and tragedy. The Roman Republic was killed by a sister republic, that of France . In that same year Marx, in his famous Communist Manifesto, launched the gospel of socialism.

In 1851 Napoleon III made his illiberal *coup d'etat* and ruled France until 1870 when he was turned out by a popular rising following one of the severest military defeats known to history. The victor was Bismarck who never even knew the whereabouts of liberalism and its prophets. It is symptomatic that throughout the XIXth century the religion of liberalism was completely unknown to so highly civilized a people as the Germans but for one parenthesis which has been described as the "ridiculous parliament of Frankfort " which lasted just one season. Germany attained her national unity outside liberalism and in opposition to liberalism, a doctrine which seems foreign to the German temperament, essentially monarchical, whereas liberalism is the historic and logical anteroom to anarchy. The three stages in the making of German unity were the three wars of 1864, 1866, and 1870, led by such "liberals" as Moltke and Bismarck. And in the upbuilding of Italian unity liberalism played a very minor part when compared to the contribution made by Mazzini and Garibaldi who were not liberals. But for the intervention of the illiberal Napoleon III we should not have had Lombardy, and without that of the illiberal Bismarck at Sadowa and at Sedan very probably we should not have had Venetia in 1866 and in 1870 we should not have entered Rome. The years going from 1870 to 1915 cover a period which marked, even in the opinion of the high priests of the new creed, the twilight of their religion, attacked by decadentism in literature and by activism in practice. Activism: that is to say nationalism, futurism, fascism.

The liberal century, after piling up innumerable Gordian Knots, tried to cut them with the sword of the world war. Never has any religion claimed so cruel a sacrifice. Were the Gods of liberalism thirsting for blood?

Now liberalism is preparing to close the doors of its temples, deserted by the peoples who feel that the agnosticism it professed in the sphere of economics and the indifferentism of which it has given proof in the sphere of politics and morals, would lead the world to ruin in the future as they have done in the past.

This explains why all the political experiments of our day are anti-liberal, and it is supremely ridiculous to endeavor on this account to put them outside the pale of history, as though history were a preserve set aside for liberalism and its adepts; as though liberalism were the last word in civilization beyond which no one can go.

The Fascist negation of socialism, democracy, liberalism, should not, however, be interpreted as implying a desire to drive the world backwards to positions occupied prior to 1789, a year commonly referred to as that which opened the demo-liberal century. History does not travel backwards. The Fascist doctrine has not taken De Maistre as its prophet.

Monarchical absolutism is of the past, and so is ecclesiolatry. Dead and done for are feudal privileges and the division of society into closed, uncommunicating castes. Neither has the Fascist conception of authority anything in common with that of a police ridden State.

A party governing a nation "totalitarianly" is a new departure in history. There are no points of reference nor of comparison. From beneath the ruins of liberal, socialist, and democratic doctrines, Fascism extracts those elements which are still vital. It preserves what may be described as "the acquired facts" of history; it rejects all else. That is to say, it rejects the idea of a doctrine suited to all times and to all people. Granted that the XIXth century was the century of socialism, liberalism, democracy, this does not mean that the XXth century must also be the century of socialism, liberalism, democracy. Political doctrines pass; nations remain. We are free to believe that this is the century of authority, a century tending to the " right ", a Fascist century. If the XIXth century was the century of the individual (liberalism implies individualism) we are free to believe that this is the "collective" century, and therefore the century of the State. It is quite logical for a new doctrine to make use of the still vital elements of other doctrines. No doctrine was ever born quite new and bright and unheard of. No doctrine can boast absolute originality. It is always connected, it only historically, with those which preceded it and those which will follow it. Thus the scientific

socialism of Marx links up to the utopian
socialism of the Fouriers, the Owens, the Saint-
Simons ; thus the liberalism of the XIXth
century traces its origin back to the illuministic
movement of the XVIIIth, and the doctrines of
democracy to those of the Encyclopaedists. All
doctrines aim at directing the activities of men
towards a given objective; but these activities in
their turn react on the doctrine, modifying and
adjusting it to new needs, or outstripping it. A
doctrine must therefore be a vital act and not a
verbal display. Hence the pragmatic strain in
Fascism, it' s will to power, its will to live, its
attitude toward violence, and its value.

The keystone of the Fascist doctrine is its
conception of the State, of its essence, its
functions, and its aims. For Fascism the State is
absolute, individuals and groups relative.
Individuals and groups are admissible in so far
as they come within the State. Instead of
directing the game and guiding the material and
moral progress of the community, the liberal
State restricts its activities to recording results.
The Fascist State is wide awake and has a will
of its own. For this reason it can be described as
" ethical ".

At the first quinquennial assembly of the
regime, in 1929, I said "The Fascist State is not
a night watchman, solicitous only of the
personal safety of the citizens; not is it
organized exclusively for the purpose of
guarantying a certain degree of material
prosperity and relatively peaceful conditions of

life, a board of directors would do as much. Neither is it exclusively political, divorced from practical realities and holding itself aloof from the multifarious activities of the citizens and the nation. The State, as conceived and realized by Fascism, is a spiritual and ethical entity for securing the political, juridical, and economic organization of the nation, an organization which in its origin and growth is a manifestation of the spirit. The State guarantees the internal and external safety of the country, but it also safeguards and transmits the spirit of the people, elaborated down the ages in its language, its customs, its faith. The State is not only the present; it is also the past and above all the future. Transcending the individual's brief spell of life, the State stands for the immanent conscience of the nation. The forms in which it finds expression change, but the need for it remains. The State educates the citizens to civism, makes them aware of their mission, urges them to unity; its justice harmonizes their divergent interests; it transmits to future generations the conquests of the mind in the fields of science, art, law, human solidarity; it leads men up from primitive tribal life to that highest manifestation of human power, imperial rule. The State hands down to future generations the memory of those who laid down their lives to ensure its safety or to obey its laws; it sets up as examples and records for future ages the names of the captains who enlarged its territory and of the men of genius who have made it famous. Whenever respect for the State declines and the disintegrating and centrifugal tendencies of individuals and groups prevail, nations are headed for decay".

Since 1929 economic and political development have everywhere emphasized these truths. The importance of the State is rapidly growing. The so-called crisis can only be settled by State action and within the orbit of the State. Where are the shades of the Jules Simons who, in the early days of liberalism proclaimed that the "State should endeavor to render itself useless and prepare to hand in its resignation "? Or of the MacCullochs who, in the second half of last century, urged that the State should desist from governing too much? And what of the English Bentham who considered that all industry asked of government was to be left alone, and of the German Humbolt who expressed the opinion that the best government was a lazy " one? What would they say now to the unceasing, inevitable, and urgently requested interventions of government in business? It is true that the second generation of economists was less uncompromising in this respect than the first, and that even Adam Smith left the door ajar - however cautiously - for government intervention in business.

If liberalism spells individualism, Fascism spells government. The Fascist State is, however, a unique and original creation. It is not reactionary but revolutionary, for it anticipates the solution of certain universal problems which have been raised elsewhere, in the political field by the splitting up of parties, the usurpation of power by parliaments, the irresponsibility of assemblies; in the economic field by the increasingly numerous and important functions discharged by trade unions and trade associations with their disputes and ententes, affecting both capital and labor; in the ethical field by the need felt for order, discipline, obedience to the moral dictates of patriotism.

Fascism desires the State to be strong and organic, based on broad foundations of popular support. The Fascist State lays claim to rule in the economic field no less than in others; it makes its action felt throughout the length and breadth of the country by means of its corporative, social, and educational institutions, and all the political, economic, and spiritual forces of the nation, organized in their respective associations, circulate within the State. A State based on millions of individuals who recognize its authority, feel its action, and are ready to serve its ends is not the tyrannical state of a mediaeval lordling. It has nothing in common with the despotic States existing prior to or subsequent to 1789. Far from crushing the individual, the Fascist State multiplies his energies, just as in a regiment a soldier is not diminished but multiplied by the number of his fellow soldiers.

The Fascist State organizes the nation, but it leaves the individual adequate elbow room. It has curtailed useless or harmful liberties while preserving those which are essential. In such matters the individual cannot be the judge, but the State only.

The Fascist State is not indifferent to religious phenomena in general nor does it maintain an attitude of indifference to Roman Catholicism, the special, positive religion of Italians. The State has not got a theology but it has a moral code. The Fascist State sees in religion one of the deepest of spiritual manifestations and for this reason it not only respects religion but defends and protects it. The Fascist State does not attempt, as did Robespierre at the height of the revolutionary delirium of the Convention, to set up a "god" of its own; nor does it vainly seek, as does Bolshevism, to efface God from the soul of man. Fascism respects the God of ascetics, saints, and heroes, and it also respects God as conceived by the ingenuous and primitive heart of the people, the God to whom their prayers are raised.

The Fascist State expresses the will to exercise power and to command. Here the Roman tradition is embodied in a conception of strength. Imperial power, as understood by the Fascist doctrine, is not only territorial, or military, or commercial; it is also spiritual and ethical. An imperial nation, that is to say a nation a which directly or indirectly is a leader of others, can exist without the need of conquering a single square mile of territory. Fascism sees in the imperialistic spirit -- i.e. in the tendency of nations to expand - a manifestation of their vitality. In the op-posite tendency, which would limit their interests to the home country, it sees a symptom of decadence. Peoples who rise or rearise are imperialistic; renunciation is characteristic of dying peoples. The Fascist doctrine is that best suited to the tendencies and feelings of a people which, like the Italian, after lying fallow during centuries of foreign servitude, are now reasserting itself in the world.

But imperialism implies discipline, the coordination of efforts, a deep sense of duty and a spirit of self-sacrifice. This explains many aspects of the practical activity of the regime, and the direction taken by many of the forces of the State, as also the severity which has to be exercised towards those who would oppose this spontaneous and inevitable movement of XXth century Italy by agitating outgrown ideologies of the XIXth century, ideologies rejected wherever great experiments in political and social transformations are being dared.

Never before have the peoples thirsted for authority, direction, order, as they do now. If each age has its doctrine, then innumerable symptoms indicate that the doctrine of our age is the Fascist. That it is vital is shown by the fact that it has aroused a faith; that this faith has conquered souls is shown by the fact that Fascism can point to its fallen heroes and its martyrs.

Fascism has now acquired throughout the world that universally which belongs to all doctrines which by achieving self-expression represent a moment in the history of human thought.

APPENDIX

1. Philosophic conception

(1) If Fascism does not wish to die or, worse still, commit suicide, it must now provide itself with a doctrine. Yet this shall not and must not be a robe of Nessus clinging to us for all eternity, for tomorrow is some thing mysterious and unforeseen. This doctrine shall be a norm to guide political and individual action in our daily life.

I who have I dictated this doctrine, am the first to realize that the modest tables of our laws and program the theoretical and practical guidance of Fascism should be revised, corrected, enlarged, developed, because already in parts they have suffered injury at the hand of time. I believe the essence and fundamentals of the doctrine are still to be found in the postulates which throughout two years have acted as a call to arms for the recruits of Italian Fascism. However, in taking those first fundamental assumptions for a starting point, we must proceed to carry our program into a vaster field.

Italian Fascists, one and all, should cooperate in this task, one of vital importance to Fascism, and more especially those who belong to regions where with and without agreement peaceful coexistence has been achieved between two antagonistic movements.

The word I am about to use is a great one, but indeed I do wish that during the two months which are still to elapse before our National Assembly meets, the philosophy of Fascism could be created. Milan is already contributing with the first Fascist school of propaganda.

It is not merely a question of gathering elements for a program, to be used as a solid foundation for the constitution of a party which must inevitably arise from the Fascist movement; it is also a question of denying the silly tale that Fascism is all made up of violent men. In point of fact among Fascists there are many men who belong to the restless but meditative class.

The new course taken by Fascist activity will in no way diminish the fighting spirit typical of Fascism. To furnish the mind with doctrines and creeds does not mean to disarm, rather it signifies to strengthen our power of action, and make us ever more conscious of our work. Soldiers who fight fully conscious of the cause make the best of warriors. Fascism takes for its own the twofold device of Mazzini : Thought and Action u. *(Letter to Michele Bianchi,* written on August 27, 1921, for the opening of the School of Fascist Culture and Propaganda in Milan, in *Messaggi e Proclami,* Milano, Libreria d'Italia, 1929, P· 39).

Fascists must be placed in contact with one another; their activity must be an activity of doctrine, an activity of the spirit and of thought . Had our adversaries been present at our meeting, they would have been convinced that Fascism is not only action, but thought as well

(Speech before the National Council of the
Fascist Party, August 8, 1924, in *La Nuova
Politica dell'Italia,* Milano,
Alpes, 1928, p. 267).

(2) Today I hold that Fascism as an idea, a
doctrine, a realization, is universal; it is Italian
in its particular institutions, but it is universal in
the spirit, nor could it be otherwise. The spirit is
universal by reason of its nature. Therefore
anyone may foresee a Fascist Europe. Drawing
inspiration for her institutions from the doctrine
and practice of Fascism; Europe , in other
words, giving a Fascist turn to the solution of
problems which beset the modern State, the
Twentieth Century State which is very different
from the States existing before 1789, and the
States formed immediately after. Today
Fascism fills universal requirements; Fascism
solves the threefold problem of relations
between State and individual, between State
and associations, between associations and
organized associations. (Message for the year 1
October 27, 1930, in *Discorsi del 1930,* Milano,
Alpes, 1931, p. 211).

2. Spiritualized conception

(3) This political process is flanked by a
philosophic process. If it be true that matter was
on the altars for one century, today it is the
spirit which takes its place. All manifestations
peculiar to the democratic spirit are
consequently repudiated: easygoingness,
improvisation, the lack of a personal sense of

responsibility,   the
exaltation of numbers and of that mysterious
divinity called n The People a. All creations of
the spirit starting with that religious are coming
to the fore, and nobody dare keep up the
attitude of anticlericalism which, for several
decades,   was   a   favorite   with
Democracy in the Western world. By saying
that God is returning, we mean that spiritual
values are returning. *(Da the parte va it mondo,
in Tempi della Rivoluzione Fascista,* Milano,
Alpes, 1930, p. 34).

There is a field reserved more to meditation
upon the supreme ends of life than to a research
of these ends. Consequently science starts from
experience, but breaks out fatally into
philosophy and, in my opinion, *philosophy*
alone can enlighten science and lead to the
universal idea. (To the Congress of Science at
Bologna , October 31, 19,26, in *Discorsi del
1926.* Milano, Alpes, 1927, p. 268).

In order to understand the Fascist movement
one must first appreciate the underlying
spiritual phenomenon in all its vastness and
depth. The manifestations of the movement
have been of a powerful and decisive nature,
but one should go further. In point of fact
Italian Fascism has not only been a political
revolt against weak and incapable governments
who had allowed State authority to decay and
were threatening to arrest the progress of the
country, but also a spiritual revolt against old
ideas which had corrupted the sacred principles
of religion, of faith, of country. Fascism,
therefore, has been a revolt of the people.

(Message to the British people; January 5, 1924, in *Messaggi e Proclami,* Milano, Libreria d' Italia, 1929, p. 107).

3 Positive conception of life as a struggle

(4) Struggle is at the origin of all things, for life is full of contrasts: there is love and hatred, white and black, day and night, good and evil; and until these contrasts achieve balance, struggle fatefully remains at the root of human nature. However, it is good for it to be so. Today we can indulge in wars, economic battles, conflicts of ideas, but if a day came to pass when struggle ceased to exist, that day would be tinged with melancholy; it would be a day of ruin, the day of ending. But that day will not come, because history ever discloses new horizons. By attempting to restore calm, peace, tranquility, or. A would be fighting the tendencies of the present period of dynamism. Ore must be prepared for other struggles and for other surprises. Peace will only come when people surrender to a Christian dream of universal brotherhood, when they can hold out hands across the ocean and over the mountains. Personally   I do not believe very much in these idealisms, but I do not exclude them for I exclude nothing. (At the Politeama Rossetti, Trieste , September *20, 1920;* in *Discorsi Politici,* Milano, Stab. Tipografico del « Popolo d' Italia » , *1921,* p. 107).

(5) For me the honor of nations consists in the contribution they have severally made to human civilization. (E. Ludwig, *Talks with Mussolini,* London, Allen and Unwin, *1932, p. 199)*

4. Ethical conception

(6) I called the organization Fasci Italiani Di combat tin onto. This hard metallic name compromised the whole program of Fascism as I dreamed it. Comrades, this is still our program: fight.

Life for the Fascist is a continuous, ceaseless fight, which we accept with ease, with great courage, with the necessary intrepidity. (C n the VIIth anniversary of the Foundation of the *Fasci,* March *2E, 1926,* in *Discorsi del 1926,* Milano, Alpes, ¹9²7, P· 9⁸**y**

You touch the core of Fascist philosophy. When recently a Finnish philosopher asked me to expound to him the significance of Fascism in one sentence, I wrote in German: ((We are against the "easy, lift! *a.* (E. Ludwig: *Talks with Mussolini,* London, Allen and Unwin, *1932, p. 190).*

5. Religious conception

(7)If Fascism were not a creed how could it endow its followers with courage and stoicism only a creed which has soared to the heights of religion can inspire such words as passed the lips, now lifeless alas, of Federico Florio. *(Legami di Sangue,* in *Diuturna, Mi*lano, Alpes, *1930, p. 256).*

6. Historical and realistic conception

(8) Tradition certainly is one of the greatest spiritual forces of a people, inasmuch as *it* is a successive and constant creation of their *soul. (Breve Preludio,* in *Tempi della Rivoluzione Fascista,* Milano, Alpes, *1930, P-13)*

(9) Our temperament leads us to appraise the concrete aspect of problems, rather than their ideological or mystical sublimation. Therefore we easily regain our balance. *(Aspetti del Dramma,* in *Diuturna,* Milano, Alpes, *1930,* p. 86).

Our battle is an ungrateful one, yet it is a beautiful battle since it compels us to count only upon our own forces. Revealed truths we have torn to shreds, dogmas we have spat upon, we have rejected all theories of paradise, we have baffled charlatans white, red, black charlatans who placed miraculous drugs on the market to give *a* happiness *n* to mankind. We do not believe in program, in plans, in saints or apostles, above all we believe not in happiness, in salvation, in the Promised Land. *(Diuturna,* Milano, Alpes, *1930, p. 223).*

We do not believe in a single solution, be it economical, political or moral, a linear solution of the problems of life, because of illustrious choristers from all the sacristies life is not linear and can never be reduced to a segment traced by primordial needs. *(Navigare necesse,* in *Diuturna,* Milano, Alpes, *1930, p. 233).*

(10) We are not and do not wish to be motionless mummies, with faces perpetually turned towards the same horizon, nor do we wish to shut ourselves up within the narrow hedges of subversive bigotry, where formulas, like prayers of a professed religion, are muttered mechanically. We are men, living men, who wish to give our contribution, however 'modest, to the creation of history. *(Audacia,* in Diu *turna,* Milano, Alpes, *1930, p. ')*

We uphold moral and traditional values which Socialism neglects or despises; but, above all, Fascism has a horror of anything implying an arbitrary mortgage on the mysterious future. *(Dopo due anni,* in *Diuturna,* Milano, Alpes, *1930, p. 242).*

In spite of the theories of conservation and renovation, of tradition and progress expounded by the right and the left, we do not cling desperately to the past as to a last board of salvation: yet we do not dash headlong into the seductive mists of the future. *(Breve preludio,* in *Diuturna,* Milano, Alpes, 1930, p. 14). [4]negation, eternal immobility, mean damnation. I am all for motion. I am, one who marches on (E. Ludwig, *Talks with Mussolini,* Lot Jon, Allen and Unwin, 1932, p. 203).

7. The individual and liberty

(11) We were the first to state, in the face of demo liberal individualism, that the individual exists only in so far as he is within the State and subjected to the requirements of the state and

that, as civilization assumes aspects which grow more and more complicated, individual freedom becomes more and more restricted. (To the General staff Conference of Fascism, in *Discorsi del 1929,* Milano, Alpes, 1930, p. 280).

The sense of the state grows within the consciousness of Italians, for they feel that the state alone is the irreplaceable safeguard of their unit and independence; that the state alone represents continuity into the future of their stock and their history. (Message on the VIIth all anniversary, October 25, 1929, *Discorsi del 1929,* Milano, Alpes, 1930, p. 3oo).

If, in the course of the past eight years, we have made such astounding progress, you may well think suppose and foresee that in the course of the next fifty or eighty years the onward trend of Italy , of this Italy we feel to be so powerful, so full of vital fluid, will really be grandiose. It will be so especially if concord lasts among citizens, if the State continues to be sole arbitrator in political and social conflicts, if all remains within the state and nothing outside the State, because it is impossible to conceive any individual existing outside the State unless he be a savage whose home is in the solitude of she sandy desert. (Speech before the Senate, May 12, 1928, in *Discorsi del 1928,* Milano, Alpes, 1929, p. 109).

Fascism has restored to the State its sovereign functions by claiming its absolute ethical meaning, against the egotism of classes and categories; to the Government of the state, which was reduced to a mere instrument of electoral assemblies, it has restored dignity, as representing the personality of the state and its power of Empire. It has rescued State administration from the weight of factions and party interests (To the council of state, December 22, 1928, in Discorsi Del 1928, Milano, Alpes, 1929 p.328).

(12)Let no one think of denying the moral character of Fascism. For I should be ashamed to speak from this tribune if I did not feel that I represent the moral and spiritual powers of the state. What would the state be if it did not possess a spirit of its own, and a morality of its own, which lend power to the laws in virtue of which the state is obeyed by its citizens?

The Fascist state claims its ethical character: it is Catholic but above all it is Fascist, in fact it is exclusively and essentially Fascist. Catholicism completes Fascism, and this we openly declare, but let no one think they can turn the tables on us, under cover of metaphysics or philosophy. (To the Chamber of Deputies, May 13, 1929, in *Discorsi del 1929,* Milano, Alpes, 1930, p. 182).

A State which is fully aware of its mission and represents a people which are marching on; a state which necessarily transforms the people even in their physical aspect. In order to be something more than a mere administrator, the State must utter great words, expound great ideas and place great problems before this people *(Di scorsi del 1929,* Milano, Alpes, 1930, p. 183).

(13)The concept of freedom is not absolute because nothing is ever absolute in life. Freedom is not a right, it is a duty. It is not a gift, it is a conquest; it is not equality, it is a privilege. The concept of freedom changes with the passing of time. There is a freedom in times of peace which is not the freedom of times of war. There is a freedom in times of prosperity which is not a freedom to be allowed in times of poverty. (Fifth anniversary of the foundation of the *Fasci di Contbattimento,* March 24, 1924, in *La nuovapolitica dell'Italia, vol.* III, Milano, Alpes, 1925, p. 30).

In our state the individual is not deprived of freedom. In fact, he has greater liberty than an isolated man, because the state protects him and he is part of the State. Isolated man is without defence. (E. Ludwig, *Talks with Mussolini,* London, Allen and Unwin, 1932, P. 129).

(14)Today we may tell the world of the creation of the powerful united State of Italy, ranging from the Alps to Sicily; this State is expressed by a well-organized, centralized, Unitarian democracy, where people circulate at case. Indeed, gentlemen, you admit the people into the citadel of the State and the people will defend it, if you close them out, the people will assault it. (speech before the Chamber of Deputies, May 26, 1927 , in *Discorsi del 1927,* Milano, Alpes, 1928, p. 159).

In the Fascist regime the unity of classes, the political, social and coral unity of the Italian people is realized within the state, and only within the Fascist state. (speech before the

Chamber of Deputies, December 9, 1928 , in *Discorsi del* 1928, Milano, Alpes, 1929, p. 333).

8. Conception of a corporative state

(15) We have created the united state of Italy remember that since the Empire Italy had not been a united state. Here I wish to reaffirm solemnly our doctrine of the State. Here I wish to reaffirm with no weaker energy, the formula I expounded at the scala in Milan everything in the state, nothing against the State, nothing outside the state. (speech before the Chamber of Deputies, May 26, 1927 , *Discorsi del 1927,* Milano, Alpes, 1928, p. t57)·

(16) We are, in other words, a state which controls all forces acting in nature. We control political forces, we control moral forces we control economic forces, therefore we are a full-blown Corporative state. We stand for a new principle in the world, we stand for sheer, categorical, definitive antithesis to the world of democracy, plutocracy, free-masonry, to the world which still abides by the fundamental principles laid down in 1789. (Speech before the new National Directory of the Party, April 7, 1926, in *Discorsi del 1926,* Milano, Alpes, 1927, p. 120).

The Ministry of Corporations is not a bureaucratic organ, nor does it wish to exercise the functions of syndical organizations which are necessarily independent, since they aim at organizing, selecting and improving the members of syndicates. The Ministry of

Corporations is an institution in virtue of which, in the centre and outside, integral corporation becomes an accomplished fact, where balance is achieved between interests and forces of the economic world. Such a glance is only possible within the sphere of the state, because the state alone transcends the contrasting interests of groups and individuals, in view of co-coordinating them to achieve higher aims. The achievement of these aims is speeded up by the fact that all economic organizations, acknowledged, safeguarded and supported by the Corporative State, exist within the orbit of Fascism; in other terms they accept the conception of Fascism in theory and in practice. (speech at the opening of the Ministry of Corporations, July 31, 1926, in *Discorsi del 1926,* Milano, Alpes, 1927, p. 250).

We have constituted a Corporative and Fascist state, the state of national society, a State which concentrates, controls, harmonizes and tempers the interests of all social classes, which are thereby protected in equal measure. Whereas, during the years of demo-liberal regime, labour looked with diffidence upon the state, was, in fact, outside the State and against the state, and considered the state an enemy of every day and every hour, there is not one working Italian today who does not seek a place in his Corporation or federation, who does not wish to be a living atom of that great, immense, living organization which is the national Corporate State of Fascism. (On the Fourth Anniversary of the March on Rome, October

28, 1926, in *Discorsi del 1926,* Milano, Alpes, 1927, p. 340).

9. Democracy

(17)The war was revolutionary, in the sense that with streams of blood it did away with the century of Democracy, the century of number, the century of majorities and of quantities. (Da *the pane va it Mondo,* in *Tempi della Rivoluzione Fascista,* Milano, Alpes, 1930, p. 37)

(18)Cf. note 13.

(19)Race: it is a feeling and not a reality; 95 %, a feeling. (E. Ludwig, *Talks with Mussolini,* London, Allen and Unwin, 1932, p. 75).

10. Conception of the state

(20)   A nation exists inasmuch as it is a people. A people rise inasmuch as they are numerous, hard working and well regulated. Power is the outcome of this threefold principle. (To the General Assembly of the Party, March lo, 1929, in *Discorsi del 1929,* Milano, Alpes, 1930, p. 24).

Fascism does not deny the State; Fascism maintains that a civic society, national or imperial, cannot be conceived unless in the form of a State *(Stab, anti-Slato, Fascismo,* in *Tempi della Rivoluzione Fascista,* Milano, Alpes, 1930' p. 94).

For us the Nation is mainly spirit and not only territory. There are States which owned immense territories and yet left no trace in the history of mankind. Neither is it a question of number, because there have been, in history, small, microscopic States, which left immortal, imperishable documents in art and philosophy.

The greatness of a nation is the compound of all these virtues and conditions. A nation is great when the power of the spirit is translated into reality. (Speech at Naples, October 24, 1922, in *Discorsi della Rivoluzione,* Milano, Alpes, 1928, p. 103). We wish to unity the nation within the sovereign State, which is above everyone arid can afford to be against everyone, since it represents the moral continuity of the nation in history. Without the State there is no nation. There are, merely. human aggregations. subject to all the disintegration's which history may inflict upon them. (Speech before the National Council of the Fascist Party, August 8, 1924, in La *Nuova Politica dell'Italia, vol.* III; Milano, Alpes, 1928, p. 269).

Dynamic reality

(21) I believe that if a people wish to live they should develop a will to power, otherwise they vegetate, live miserably and become prey to a stronger people, in whom this will to power is developed to a higher degree. (Speech to the Senate, May 28, 1926).

(22) It is Fascism which has refashioned the character of the Italians, removing impurity from our souls, tempering us to all sacrifices, restoring the true aspect of strength and beauty to our Italian face. (Speech delivered at Pisa , May 25, 1926 , *in Discorsi del 1926,* Milano, Alpes, 1927, p. 193).

It is not out of place to illustrate the intrinsic character and profound significance of the Fascist Levy. It is not merely a ceremony, but a very important stage in the system of education and integral preparation of Italian men which the Fascist revolution considers one of the fundamental duties of the State: fundamental indeed, for if the State does not fulfill this duty or in any way accepts to place it under discussion, the State merely and simply forfeits its right to exist. (Speech before the Chamber of Deputies, May 28, 1928, in *Discorsi del 1928,* Milano, Alpes, 1929, p. 68).

Printed in the USA
CPSIA information can be obtained
at www.ICGtesting.com
LVHW021341171023
761356LV00004B/29